40 Minute
BIBLE STUDIES

6-WEEK
STUDY PROGRAM

BEING A

DISCIPLE:

COUNTING

THE REAL

COST

PRECEPT
MINISTRIES
INTERNATIONAL

KAY ARTHUR
TOM & JANE HART

BEING A DISCIPLE: COUNTING THE REAL COST
PUBLISHED BY WATERBROOK PRESS
2375 Telstar Drive, Suite 160
Colorado Springs, Colorado 80920
A division of Random House, Inc.

All Scripture quotations, unless otherwise indicated, are taken from the *New American Standard Bible*® (NASB), © Copyright The Lockman Foundation 1960, 1962, 1963, 1968, 1971, 1972, 1973, 1975, 1977, 1995. Used by permission. (www.Lockman.org)

Italics in Scripture quotations reflect the author's added emphasis.

ISBN 1-57856-476-X

Copyright © 2001 by Precept Ministries International

All rights reserved. No part of this book may be reproduced or transmitted in any form or by any means, electronic or mechanical, including photocopying and recording, or by any information storage and retrieval system, without permission in writing from the publisher.

WATERBROOK and its deer design logo are registered trademarks of WaterBrook Press, a division of Random House, Inc.

Printed in the United States of America
2002

10 9 8 7 6 5

This small-group study is for people who are interested in learning more about what the Bible says, but who have only limited time to meet together. It's ideal, for example, for a lunch group at work, an early morning men's group, a young mother's group meeting in a home, or a smaller Sunday-school class. (It's also ideal for small groups that typically have longer meeting times—such as evening groups or Saturday morning groups—but want to devote only a portion of their time together to actual study, while reserving the rest for prayer, fellowship, or other activities.)

This book is designed so that all the group's participants will complete each lesson's study activities *at the same time, while you're together.*

However, you'll need a facilitator to lead the group—someone to keep the discussion moving. (This person's function is *not* that of a lecturer or teacher. However, when this book is used in a Sunday-school class or similar setting, the teacher should feel free to lead more directly and to bring in other insights in addition to those provided in each week's lesson.)

If *you* are your group's facilitator, the leader, here are some helpful points for making your job easier:

- Go through the lesson and mark the text before you lead the group. This will give you increased familiarity with the material and will enable you to facilitate the group with greater ease. It may be easier for you to lead the group through the instructions for marking if you as a leader choose a specific color for each symbol you mark.
- As you lead the group, start at the beginning of the text and simply read it aloud in the order it appears in the lesson,

including the "insight boxes," which may appear either before or after the instructions or in the midst of your observations or discussion. Work through the lesson together, observing and discussing what you learn. As you read the Scripture verses, have the group say aloud the word they are marking in the text.

- The discussion questions are there simply to help you cover the material. As the class moves into the discussion, many times you will find that they will cover the questions on their own. Remember the discussion questions are there to guide the group through the topic, not to squelch discussion.

- Remember how important it is for people to verbalize their answers and discoveries. This greatly strengthens their personal understanding of each week's lesson. Try to ensure that everyone has plenty of opportunity to contribute to each week's discussions.

- Keep the discussion moving. This may mean spending more time on some parts of the study than on others. If necessary, you should feel free to spread out a lesson over more than one session. However, remember that you don't want to slow the pace too much. It's much better to leave everyone "wanting more" than to have people dropping out because of declining interest.

- If the validity or accuracy of some of the answers seems questionable, you can gently and cheerfully remind the group to stay focused on the truth of the Scriptures. Your object is to learn what the Bible says, not to engage in human philosophy. Really *read* the Scriptures, asking God to show everyone His answers.

BEING A DISCIPLE: COUNTING THE REAL COST

When Jesus called men and women to follow Him, what did He expect of them? And was it reasonable? What's the difference between those who say they're Christians and everyone else? What proves whether a person is a true disciple of Jesus Christ or not?

These are the questions we want to answer as we search out what the Bible has to say about the subject of being a disciple of Jesus Christ. We are going to take an *inductive* approach, which means that you will observe the Word of God for yourself. Then, discovering what it says and means, you can determine if you want to order your life according to its truth.

Most people are followers of someone. Someone catches their attention, captures their imagination, or shares the same interests and values. Consequently they want to know more about that person—the goals he or she is pursuing, the accomplishments attained. They want to talk and learn from this person. And if what they find is pleasing or applicable to their desires and ambitions, they want to emulate him, pursue his interests, or take up his cause.

Basically we are followers of those who have gone before us or those who have achieved what we want to achieve. This may be our parents, our peers, our teachers, or our heroes in the realms of our interest—but there is usually someone we want to be like because we believe in who he is or what he is about.

A disciple is a follower. Moses had disciples, the Pharisees had disciples, John the Baptist had disciples.

When Jesus began His public ministry, He, too, looked for disciples so that, when His work was finished and He left to be with the Father again, there would be others who would faithfully carry on the work of the kingdom of God—a kingdom that was now at hand.

OBSERVE

As we begin, let's look at a passage that shows us how Jesus called His first disciples.

Leader: Read aloud Matthew 4:17-22.

• *Mark the word **follow** by underlining it and putting an arrow on the end of the line, like this:* ⟶

MATTHEW 4:17-22

17 From that time Jesus began to preach and say, "Repent, for the kingdom of heaven is at hand."

18 Now as Jesus was walking by the Sea of

Galilee, He saw two brothers, Simon who was called Peter, and Andrew his brother, casting a net into the sea; for they were fishermen.

19 And He said to them, "Follow Me, and I will make you fishers of men."

20 Immediately they left their nets and followed Him.

21 Going on from there He saw two other brothers, James the son of Zebedee, and John his brother, in the boat with Zebedee their father, mending their nets; and He called them.

22 Immediately they left the boat and their father, and followed Him.

DISCUSS

• When Jesus asked them to follow Him, what did He say He would make them?

• What had they been doing?

• What do you think Jesus meant by "fishers of men"?

Leader: *Have the group share in fifteen seconds or less what some of them were doing when Jesus first called them to believe on Him. Why did they follow Him?*

OBSERVE

The pond from which the disciples were going to fish was the world! You might say this was the private lake of the devil—or so the devil thought! But Jesus knew He had many fish who needed to be netted into the kingdom of God.

Leader: In Matthew 10:16-22, we have a portion of Jesus' instructions to the twelve disciples (whom He also appointed as apostles) before He sent them to the lost sheep of the house of Israel. Read the passage aloud and have the group...

- circle every (instruction) that Jesus gives them.
- underline everything that is going to **happen** to them.

DISCUSS

- Does what Jesus said sound very appealing or attractive?

- What are the things that can or will happen to them as His disciples? Talk about what you have underlined.

- What are Jesus' instructions?

MATTHEW 10:16-22

16 "Behold, I send you out as sheep in the midst of wolves; so be shrewd as serpents and innocent as doves.

17 "But beware of men, for they will hand you over to the courts and scourge you in their synagogues;

18 and you will even be brought before governors and kings for My sake, as a testimony to them and to the Gentiles.

19 "But when they hand you over, do not worry about how or what you are to say; for it will be given you in that hour what you are to say.

20 "For it is not you who speak, but it is the Spirit of your Father who speaks in you.

21 "Brother will betray brother to death, and a father his child; and children will rise up against parents and cause them to be put to death.

22 "You will be hated by all because of My name, but it is the one who has endured to the end who will be saved."

• Are there any assurances? promises of help?

• Would you say Jesus was "up front" about what it means to follow Him? Why?

• If those things were going to happen to you, would you still want to follow Jesus?

• Do you realize that these things are happening to many Christians around the world today? And it has happened in every age—beginning with the first twelve of His disciples!

OBSERVE

Leader: Read aloud Matthew 10:24-31.

- *Mark every reference to* **disciple,** *including pronouns, in the same way you marked "follow" by underlining it and putting an arrow on the end of the line.*
- *Mark every occurrence of the word* **fear** *with a series of short lines.*

DISCUSS

- What did Jesus teach them about a disciple's relationship to his master?

- What were they not to fear? What were they supposed to fear? (List these under the headings provided.)

Not to Fear

To Fear

MATTHEW 10:24-31

24 "A disciple is not above his teacher, nor a slave above his master.

25 "It is enough for the disciple that he become like his teacher, and the slave like his master. If they have called the head of the house Beelzebul, how much more will they malign the members of his household!

26 "Therefore do not fear them, for there is nothing concealed that will not be revealed, or hidden that will not be known.

27 "What I tell you in the darkness, speak in the light; and what you hear whispered in your ear, proclaim upon the housetops.

28 "Do not fear those who kill the body but are unable to kill the soul; but rather fear Him who is able to destroy both soul and body in hell.

29 "Are not two sparrows sold for a cent? And yet not one of them will fall to the ground apart from your Father.

30 "But the very hairs of your head are all numbered.

31 "So do not fear; you are more valuable than many sparrows."

• What are the reasons they shouldn't fear? What can the disciples be assured of?

Leader: When answering this last question, make sure the group looks at verse 29 very carefully. Don't miss "apart from your Father"—which means, "without His knowledge and therefore His permission"! Follow this point by tying in verses 30-31.

• What are Jesus' instructions in this passage? What are His disciples to do?

Leader: Read aloud the Insight Box.

INSIGHT

Beelzebul is a name of Satan. Some accused Jesus of being from the devil, Satan. If they accused Jesus of this, then the disciples could expect to be accused of the same.

OBSERVE

Jesus has more to say to His disciples, so let's continue with Matthew 10:32-40.

Leader: *Read aloud Matthew 10:32-40.*
- *Circle the words **everyone**, **whoever**, and **He.***
- *Mark with a cross every reference to **Jesus**, including pronouns:* †
- *Mark **therefore** with three dots in the form of a triangle:* ∴

DISCUSS

- *Therefore* is a term of conclusion—a kind of wrapping up of a thought. As you read this portion, did you see a change in what was being said? a conclusion? What is happening in verses 32-40?

- What is the contrast between the "everyone" and the "whoever" in verses 32-33? And what is Jesus' response to both?

MATTHEW 10:32-40

32 "Therefore everyone who confesses Me before men, I will also confess him before My Father who is in heaven.

33 "But whoever denies Me before men, I will also deny him before My Father who is in heaven.

34 "Do not think that I came to bring peace on the earth; I did not come to bring peace, but a sword.

35 "For I came to set a man against his father, and a daughter against her mother, and a daughter-in-law against her mother-in-law;

36 and a man's enemies will be the members of his household.

37 "He who loves father or mother more than Me is not worthy of Me; and he who loves son or daughter more than Me is not worthy of Me.

38 "And he who does not take his cross and follow after Me is not worthy of Me.

39 "He who has found his life will lose it, and he who has lost his life for My sake will find it.

40 "He who receives you receives Me, and he who receives Me receives Him who sent Me."

• Does this seem hard on Jesus' part, or reasonable? Does it matter whether it is reasonable or not?

• What does Jesus want His disciples to understand in verses 34-37? Is this the first time you've read this? What is clarified even more about the disciples' relationship to Jesus Christ?

• What does it take to have this kind of allegiance to Jesus Christ? What is the promise of such commitment? (Look closely at verses 38-39.)

• In verse 40, what do you learn about the relationship between Jesus and His disciples? About Jesus' relationship with the Father?

Leader: *Read aloud the Insight Box.*

INSIGHT

The Greek word translated as *disciple* comes from a verb that means "to learn." A disciple attached himself to another to gain practical or theoretical knowledge by instruction or experience. It was a word used of apprentices learning a trade as well as students learning a teacher's philosophy.

Discipleship was a popular concept in the Jewish religion of Jesus' day. Customarily, disciples left home and moved in with their teacher, who provided their food and lodging. The disciples became his servants and were under his total authority. They were to learn everything the teacher knew—becoming like him in character—and were later to faithfully transmit this to others.

WRAP IT UP

Honestly, how do you feel when you read these scriptures we've looked at this week?

How relevant do you think they are to today?

Do you think these things pertained only to the twelve disciples of Jesus—or could they possibly apply to us?

These are strong teachings, aren't they? Have you ever wondered if *every* Christian is called to be a disciple—and if so, how such knowledge and understanding of Jesus' requirements for disciples might change the way we present the Lord Jesus Christ to others? What do you think?

Talk to God about it—ask Him what He thinks…

The twelve disciples were just the beginning. Jesus wanted others to follow Him, to be His disciples.

When Jesus called men and women to follow Him, what did He expect of them? And was it reasonable?

This week we are going to look at other passages that deal with what it means to be a disciple of Jesus Christ—the cost of following Him.

OBSERVE

Leader: Read aloud Mark 8:34-38, reprinted in the sidebars on pages 14 and 15. Have the group say aloud the words they will mark when you read them.

- *Jesus is speaking in this passage; therefore mark with a cross every pronoun referring to Him, such as **He, Me, My, His.***
- *Mark **disciples** by underlining it and putting an arrow at the end of the line, like this:* ➡
- *Mark **anyone** (and all the pronouns or synonyms that relate to "anyone") with a big **A**.*

DISCUSS

- To whom is Jesus speaking in these verses?

MARK 8:34-38

34 And He summoned the crowd with His disciples, and said to them, "If anyone wishes to come after Me, he must deny① himself, and take up his cross and follow Me.

35 "For whoever wishes to save his life will lose it, but whoever loses his life for My sake and the gospel's will save it.

36 "For what does it profit a man to gain the whole world, and forfeit his soul?

37 "For what will a man give in exchange for his soul?

• When Jesus said, "If anyone wishes to come after Me," the Greek tense of the verb *come* implies continuous or habitual action. Jesus wasn't talking about a casual walk. In light of this and of what you've learned about a disciple, do you think Jesus was talking about being His disciple when He used this phrase? Give the reason for your answer.

• If a person chose to come after Jesus, what specific things must he or she do? Put a number (1,2,3) with a circle around it near each of the points in the text. See the example in verse 34.

Leader: *Read aloud the Insight Box.*

INSIGHT

The cross was a torturous instrument of execution used by the Romans for slaves and foreigners. All Roman citizens were exempted from crucifixion, which was considered a disgraceful way to die. Those who were to be crucified were often required to carry the cross, or at least its crossbar, to the place of crucifixion. The site of crucifixion was usually along a well-traveled road, where criminals became a public spectacle. Their humiliation by such a death could be seen by all.

The verb forms for "deny" and "take up" are in the aorist tense, which simply implies action at a point of time. In other words, this is something you decide and then do.

The verb translated as "follow" is in the present tense and denotes habitual or continual action. So once you deny yourself and take up your cross, the habit of your life will be to follow Jesus continuously.

38 "For whoever is ashamed of Me and My words in this adulterous and sinful generation, the Son of Man will also be ashamed of him when He comes in the glory of His Father with the holy angels."

DISCUSS

• When Jesus called the disciples to take up their cross, what in essence was He saying to them?

• How does denying yourself and taking up your cross relate to losing your life for Jesus' sake and the gospel's?

• And what about those who refuse to follow Jesus because of the cost? What do you learn about them from this text?

• Who will the Son of Man be ashamed of when He comes in His glory with the holy angels? Why? What were they ashamed of? Where?

• Stop and think about where this person was ashamed of Jesus and of His words. What kind of people's praise and approval did this person choose over Jesus Christ? Stop and think of this when you are tempted to play the coward before the world instead of standing for Jesus Christ—and for His Word.

• Do you believe Jesus requires the same today for those who desire "to come after Him"—or is this for some elite group of believers?

• Is there anything that keeps you from denying yourself? Is it worth it?

• If Jesus were standing before you today, saying the same thing, how would you respond to an invitation like this?

OBSERVE

Leader: Read aloud Luke 14:25-27. Have the group...

    • *mark every occurrence of* **disciple.**
    • *put a cross over every reference to* **Jesus.** *He is the one speaking in this passage.*

DISCUSS

• To whom is Jesus speaking in this passage?

• What is the subject?

LUKE 14:25-27

25 Now large crowds were going along with Him; and He turned and said to them,

26 "If anyone comes to Me, and does not hate his own father and mother and wife and children and brothers and sisters, yes, and even his own life, he cannot be My disciple.

27 "Whoever does not carry his own cross and come after Me cannot be My disciple."

• What are the conditions Jesus lays down for being a disciple?

Leader: *You may want the group to list these conditions for quick reference or to number them in the text.*

• If God is love and He tells us to love not only one another but also our enemies, do you think Jesus is saying that in order to be His disciple you must literally hate your parents, mate, children, and relatives? Give reasons for your answer.

• Could it be that *hate* here is being used as hyperbole (deliberate exaggeration for effect or emphasis)? That our love for others should be like hatred in comparison of—what?

• What does it mean to hate your own life?

• What does this show you about a disciple's allegiance to Jesus Christ?

• Does all this seem like too high a cost to you for following Jesus?

OBSERVE

Leader: *Continue by reading Luke 14:28-33.*
- *Mark any reference to **Jesus,** who is speaking, with a cross.*
- *Mark every occurrence of **disciple.***

DISCUSS

- Jesus is speaking to the multitudes and He has just told them what they are to do if they are going to come to Him, to be His disciples. Now what is He urging them to do in verses 28-33 and why?

- Are they to make the decision about following Him lightly? Is it a "light decision"? Why not? What must anyone do who wants to follow Jesus, to be His disciple? Spell it out the way Jesus does in this passage.

- *So then* in verse 33 is a term of conclusion. What's the conclusion of what Jesus said? What does this tell you about the place Jesus is to have in a disciple's life?

LUKE 14:28-33

28 "For which one of you, when he wants to build a tower, does not first sit down and calculate the cost to see if he has enough to complete it?

29 "Otherwise, when he has laid a foundation and is not able to finish, all who observe it begin to ridicule him,

30 saying, 'This man began to build and was not able to finish.'

31 "Or what king, when he sets out to meet another king in battle, will not first sit down and consider whether he is strong enough with ten thousand men to encounter

the one coming
against him with
twenty thousand?

32 "Or else, while the
other is still far away,
he sends a delegation
and asks for terms of
peace.

33 "So then, none of
you can be My disciple
who does not give up
all his own possessions."

Leader: Read aloud the Insight Box.

INSIGHT

The verb "give up" in Luke 14:33 literally means to say good-bye (by departing or dismissing); figuratively it means to renounce. In other words, it means that you are willing to hold everything you have in an open hand. If God wants it, He can have it. You may possess some-thing—own it—but it does not pos-sess you. You are willing to let it go if necessary in order to follow Jesus Christ.

LUKE 12:51-53

51 "Do you suppose
that I came to grant
peace on earth? I tell
you, no, but rather
division;

OBSERVE

Leader: Read aloud Luke 12:51-53.

- *Jesus is speaking here; mark every pro-noun that refers to Him with a cross.*
- *Mark the words division and divided with a slash after the "v", like this:* div/ision

DISCUSS

• According to these verses, what does Jesus bring? Among whom?

• Why? What would bring division?

• Do you think it would bring division if one member of the family decided to be a disciple of Jesus Christ—deny himself or herself, take up his or her cross, and follow Jesus forever—and the other members didn't want to do that?

• Do you know of anyone who experienced opposition or rejection from his or her family after becoming a Christian? It happens all over the world, especially when family members are from a different faith, such as Islam or Hinduism.

52 for from now on five members in one household will be divided, three against two and two against three.

53 "They will be divided, father against son and son against father, mother against daughter and daughter against mother, mother-in-law against daughter-in-law and daughter-in-law against mother-in-law."

WRAP IT UP

Discuss what you learned these past two weeks about those who would be disciples of Jesus Christ.

Have you ever really stopped to consider the "cost" of being a disciple of Jesus Christ?

It would be good to close this week's study with a time of prayer, discussing what you have learned with the Father and the Son—who, after all, are the Ones laying down the requirements of such commitment.

Have you ever looked at people who claim to be Christians—believers in Jesus Christ—and you weren't impressed at all with their lives? Maybe you thought, "If that's a Christian I'm not sure I want to be one." Or maybe you wondered, "What's the difference between those who say they're Christians and everyone else?"

And what about those who work miracles, cast out demons, and speak for God? Is that concrete evidence that they are Christians?

This week we are going to look at several different groups of people and find out what Jesus Christ had to say about them and about who is really His true follower and going to heaven.

DISCUSS

• How does society in general look at Christians? What do people think about them and the image they project? Are there any distinctives, positive or negative, that describe Christians?

• When you look at people who call themselves Christians, what is your general impression of them?

OBSERVE

Is it possible for a person to think he or she is a Christian and on the way to heaven, yet be deceived?

Let's examine what Jesus said to some of His followers one day on a grassy mount overlooking the Sea of Galilee. It's the conclusion of a message Jesus gave to His disciples and others who were drawn to Him because of all the amazing things they heard Him say and saw Him do.

MATTHEW 7:13-14

13 "Enter through the narrow gate; for the gate is wide and the way is broad that leads to destruction, and there are many who enter through it.

14 "For the gate is small and the way is narrow that leads to life, and there are few who find it."

Leader: Have the group read Matthew 7:13-14 aloud. Then have them read through it again on their own and list under the headings "Narrow Gate" and "Wide Gate" what they learn from the text about these two different gates and those who enter through them.

Narrow Gate

Wide Gate

DISCUSS

• What do you learn about these two gates?

• How do they differ?

• Where do they lead?

• Who is walking through them?

OBSERVE

Leader: Read aloud Matthew 7:15-23.

- *Mark every reference to* **false prophets** *(including synonyms and pronouns) with a large* **X**. *When you come to the word* **prophesy,** *put an* **X** *over it and circle it.*

- *Mark every reference to* **fruit** *with this symbol:* 🍎

  To distinguish the bad fruit from the good, put a slash through the bad fruit, like this: 🍎

Leader: Before you discuss what you observed in the text, read aloud the Insight Box.

INSIGHT

False prophets claimed to be spokesmen for God. Like true prophets, they would deliver a message supposedly from God to the people that dealt with either the present situation or with the future.

(continued on next page)

MATTHEW 7:15-23

15 "Beware of the false prophets, who come to you in sheep's clothing, but inwardly are ravenous wolves.

16 "You will know them by their fruits. Grapes are not gathered from thorn bushes nor figs from thistles, are they?

17 "So every good tree bears good fruit, but the bad tree bears bad fruit.

18 "A good tree cannot produce bad fruit, nor can a bad tree produce good fruit.

19 "Every tree that does not bear good fruit is cut down and thrown into the fire.

(continued from page 25)

Throughout the Scriptures you'll find references to true prophets, such as Daniel, Ezekiel, and Jeremiah, who had genuine messages from God. There are also many references to false prophets who would deliver messages or relate dreams and visions that were not from God. False prophets often brought messages that were contrary to those of the true prophets. Their messages were often more appealing, because people would rather hear positive messages that promise good things than messages that warn of judgment and call people to repentance and righteousness. The true prophets confronted sin; the false whitewashed it.

The dilemma facing the people was this: How could you tell a true prophet from a false prophet?

DISCUSS

• What do you learn about false prophets from marking the text?

• What are the false prophets likened to in verse 15?

• According to Jesus, how does a person recognize a false prophet? How will you know a false prophet?

• According to the verses you just read, what shows a person whether a tree is good or bad?

• Would a false prophet claim to be going to heaven—or maybe even think he's going to heaven?

• Would he or she claim to know the way to heaven?

• What do the "many" in verse 22 think, and why?

• What does Jesus tell them, and why?

20 "So then, you will know them by their fruits.

21 "Not everyone who says to Me, 'Lord, Lord,' will enter the kingdom of heaven, but he who does the will of My Father who is in heaven will enter.

22 "Many will say to Me on that day, 'Lord, Lord, did we not prophesy in Your name, and in Your name cast out demons, and in Your name perform many miracles?'

23 "And then I will declare to them, 'I never knew you; depart from Me, you who practice lawlessness.'"

• According to verse 21, who is going to enter the kingdom of heaven?

• Who is going to be told to depart from Jesus because He *never* knew them? How are they described in verse 23?

• Do you see any correlation between bad fruit and practicing lawlessness?

MATTHEW 7:13-15,22

13 "Enter through the narrow gate; for the gate is wide and the way is broad that leads to destruction, and there are many who enter through it.

14 "For the gate is small and the way is narrow that leads to life, and there are few who find it.

OBSERVE

Leader: Read aloud Matthew 7:13-15,22 again and have the group underline the commands.

DISCUSS

• What are the two commands Jesus gives His listeners in these verses?

• Do you see any correlation between these two warnings?

OBSERVE

Leader: *Read aloud Matthew 7:13 and 7:22 to the group.*

- *Have the group say the word **many** when you read it and have them mark it with a squiggly line, like this:*

  ~~~~~~~

- *In verse 22, what three things did the "many" claim to have done? Have the group put a number (1,2,3) with a circle around it near each of the points in the text.*

DISCUSS

- What do you observe from marking *many*?

- Do you see any correlation between the illustration of the two gates, the illustration of the two trees, and the false prophets?

- Which gate do you think the false prophets would lead people to? Why?

15 "Beware of the false prophets, who come to you in sheep's clothing, but inwardly are ravenous wolves....

22 "Many will say to Me on that day, 'Lord, Lord, did we not prophesy in Your name, and in Your name cast out demons, and in Your name perform many miracles?'"

MATTHEW 7:24-29

24 "Therefore everyone who hears these words of Mine and acts on them, may be compared to a wise man who built his house on the rock.

25 "And the rain fell, and the floods came, and the winds blew and slammed against that house; and yet it did not fall, for it had been founded on the rock.

26 "Everyone who hears these words of Mine and does not act on them, will be like a foolish man who built his house on the sand.

OBSERVE

Leader: Read aloud Matthew 7:24-29. Have the group say "wise man" when you come to that phrase in the text and say "foolish man" when you come to it.

- *Put a box around the references to the **wise man** and the **foolish man**. However, put a slash through the box for the foolish man, like this:*
- *Underline every occurrence of the phrase **everyone who hears these words of Mine**.*

DISCUSS

- What do you learn about the wise man and the foolish man? about their houses? where they build? how they withstand storms?

- Why do you think Jesus used the illustration of rain, flood, and wind? In this same message Jesus gave, He said: "Blessed are those who have been persecuted for the sake of righteousness, for theirs is the kingdom of heaven. Blessed are you when people insult you and persecute you, and falsely say all kinds of evil against you because of Me. Rejoice and be glad, for your reward in heaven is great; for in the same way they persecuted the prophets who were before you" (Matthew 5:10-12). Do you see any possible parallel between the persecution and the rain, flood, and wind? What enables one house to stand and causes the other to fall?

• What distinguishes the wise from the foolish? What makes someone foolish?

• What did you observe when you underlined "everyone who hears these words of Mine"?

• Jesus mentioned two gates, two kinds of trees, and now two kinds of men—all to illustrate truth. Is there any comparison between the two gates, the two trees, and the two men? Any similarities? What are they?

• According to the passage you're studying, if you believed a false prophet instead of Jesus, the true Prophet, where would it lead you?

27 "The rain fell, and the floods came, and the winds blew and slammed against that house; and it fell—and great was its fall."

28 When Jesus had finished these words, the crowds were amazed at His teaching;

29 for He was teaching them as one having authority, and not as their scribes.

WRAP IT UP

It's important to stop and consider how all this applies to us. What are the lessons we can learn from this text?

First of all we need to see that fruit and deeds are synonymous. Fruit is what your life produces. Bad fruit is not an occasional rotten apple hanging on your limb—rather it is the totality of the fruit that shows what the tree is really like. The root produces the fruit!

The ones who thought they were going to heaven—who called Jesus "Lord," and who cast out demons, prophesied in His name, and did miracles—were not going to heaven because they practiced lawlessness. This was their lifestyle. Their fruit. They heard the words of Jesus, but they did not act on them.

They took a broad way through a wide gate and found that it led to destruction: "I never knew you; depart from Me."

They built their house on sand because they heard Jesus' words but they did not act on them. Their deeds, their fruit was not the righteousness of obedience—it was lawlessness.

So what is God's word to you? What has He taught you?

What are the two commands you looked at? Review them.

What do you need to do? Share what God taught you—or confirmed in these last thirty-five minutes or so.

Can a person prophesy in Jesus' name, cast out demons, perform miracles, and *not* go to heaven? How do you know? Then should you be awed by these things when you see or hear of them? What should you examine? Why?

How important is it that you listen to the right person? follow the right person?

How important is it to know the Word of God for yourself?

Do you see any parallels between what you studied this week and what you studied the last two weeks?

These are not easy verses of Scripture to look at, are they? We know that this is a confrontational study—but the rewards are great!

These are critical passages if you want a biblical understanding of what salvation and being a disciple are all about. They are heavy truths—truths you want to think about, pray about, and possibly study even further in the future.

(Kay Arthur has written two in-depth "Lord" studies on the Sermon on the Mount—*Lord, Only You Can Change Me* on the beatitudes and *Lord, I'm Torn Between Two Masters* on the rest of the Sermon on the Mount. You might want to consider studying these as a group when you have time to do homework on your own during the week.)

We have looked at the call of a disciple and the cost of discipleship. Now we want to look at the commitment of a disciple.

What proves whether a person is a true disciple of Jesus Christ or not? Is it possible to be a disciple, a learner, a follower for a while, and not be a true believer in the Lord Jesus Christ and thereby miss the gift of eternal life and instead spend eternity in the lake of fire?

This is what we want to look at this week.

OBSERVE

By the third year of Jesus' ministry, His popularity was waning. Opposition was increasing. In John 6 we read that, as Jesus taught in the synagogue in Capernaum, He made it explicitly clear that He was the living bread sent by the living Father and that only those who ate His flesh and drank His blood would abide in Him and live forever. In other words, abiding (continuing, remaining) in Jesus was the only means to eternal life.

Jesus' words were not well received by all.

Leader: *Read aloud John 6:60-71.*

- *Mark every occurrence of the word **disciples** (including any relative pronouns or synonyms, such as **the twelve**).*

JOHN 6:60-71

60 Therefore many of His disciples, when they heard this said, "This is a difficult statement; who can listen to it?"

61 But Jesus, conscious that His disciples grumbled at this, said to them, "Does this cause you to stumble?

62 "What then if you see the Son of Man ascending to where He was before?

63 "It is the Spirit who gives life; the flesh profits nothing; the words that I have spoken to you are spirit and are life.

64 "But there are some of you who do not believe." For Jesus knew from the beginning who they were who did not believe, and who it was that would betray Him.

65 And He was saying, "For this reason I have said to you, that no one can come to Me unless it has been granted him from the Father."

66 As a result of this many of His disciples withdrew and were not walking with Him anymore.

• *Put a big **B** over every occurrence of the word **believe**.*

DISCUSS

• What is the atmosphere in verses 60-61 and why?

• Move through the text verse by verse and discuss what you learn in each one about the disciples. What's the problem in verse 64?

• What do you learn about Jesus' words in verse 63? According to this passage, how did some of Jesus' disciples respond to what He said? If you miss Jesus' words—don't believe them—what are you missing?

• Look at verse 66. Why did many disciples withdraw—not walk with Jesus anymore? Consider the whole context of verses 60-66 for your answer.

• Did Jesus alter His message, soften it, adjust it so they would stay? What does this tell you about our responsibility—the responsibility of the church when people come inquiring about Jesus Christ and Christianity?

• What about the Twelve? What do you learn about them?

• What other verse does verse 68 parallel?

• What does this tell you about the importance of the Word of God? its value? its power?

• If someone were to ask you if it is possible to call yourself a disciple of Jesus Christ and not really be a true follower of His, what would your answer be, according to this passage?

OBSERVE

Let's see what Jesus says about true discipleship.

67 So Jesus said to the twelve, "You do not want to go away also, do you?"

68 Simon Peter answered Him, "Lord, to whom shall we go? You have words of eternal life.

69 "We have believed and have come to know that You are the Holy One of God."

70 Jesus answered them, "Did I Myself not choose you, the twelve, and yet one of you is a devil?"

71 Now He meant Judas the son of Simon Iscariot, for he, one of the twelve, was going to betray Him.

JOHN 8:31

So Jesus was saying to those Jews who had believed Him, "If you continue in My word, then you are truly disciples of Mine."

Leader: *Have the group read aloud with you John 8:31.*
- *Mark the references to **disciples.***
- *Mark **believe** with a big **B.***
- *Circle the word **if**, and double underline the phrase **truly disciples of mine.***

Leader: *Read aloud the Insight Box.*

INSIGHT

The verb translated as *continue* in John 8:31 means to remain or stay (in a given place, state, relation, or expectancy). It is also translated in some English versions as *abide.* It is presented in the Greek of this verse as a conditional statement—"*If* you continue"—something that remains to be seen. The text is saying that if you remain or continue in Jesus' teaching then it proves you're a genuine disciple. The validation of true discipleship is to not depart from the Word of God, but to continue in it...to keep on believing, to keep on following, and thus ordering your life accordingly.

DISCUSS

• To whom is Jesus speaking in John 8:31?

• What does the text tell you about them?

• What is Jesus' admonition to them? What is the commitment of a true disciple?

OBSERVE

Chapters 13 through 16 of the gospel of John are often referred to as the "Upper Room Discourse." In John 13 we have an account of Jesus' final celebration of the Passover, commonly called the "Last Supper." This account tells of Judas's betrayal of Jesus. Judas's commitment ended. He would not "abide," remain faithful to Jesus Christ. He would deny Him as the Christ for thirty pieces of silver.

After Judas left the Upper Room, Jesus spoke to the eleven who remained.

John 13:34-35

34 "A new commandment I give to you, that you love one another, even as I have loved you, that you also love one another.

35 "By this all men will know that you are My disciples, if you have love for one another."

Leader: Read aloud John 13:34-35.

- *Mark again any reference to the **disciples.***
- *Put a heart over every mention of **love,** like this:* ♡
- *Circle the phrase* (even as.)

DISCUSS

- According to these verses, what proves to others that a person is a disciple of Jesus Christ?

- In general does love characterize those who claim to know Jesus Christ today?

- The Law said we were to love others as ourselves, but now love is taken to a new plane. How are we to love others now?

- To what extent did Jesus love us? Do you see any parallel here to denying self and taking up the cross? Any parallel to the narrow road, the small gate, the few?

- Did Judas meet this qualification? How do you know?

OBSERVE

We are now going to look at John 15, but first let's put ourselves into context. In chapters 13 and 14 of John, Jesus is still in the Upper Room with His disciples. Judas leaves to betray Him. John 14 closes with this statement from Jesus: "Get up, let us go from here." Jesus and His eleven disciples then leave the Upper Room to proceed to the Garden of Gethsemane on the Mount of Olives, where Jesus will eventually be arrested after Judas betrays Him with a kiss.

Eleven of the twelve have remained faithful—one has walked away. Judas didn't walk away in John 6, when Jesus turned to the Twelve and said, "Will you go away also?" However, he has now!

Judas chose not to abide, not to remain in his relationship with Jesus Christ.

This, we believe, is what prompted Jesus to teach what it means to abide and what happens if you don't.

Leader: Read aloud through John 15:1-8. This is an allegory. An allegory is like an extended metaphor; it's a description of one thing using the image of another.

JOHN 15:1-8

1 "I am the true vine, and My Father is the vinedresser.

2 "Every branch in Me that does not bear fruit, He takes away; and every branch that bears fruit, He prunes it so that it may bear more fruit.

3 "You are already clean because of the word which I have spoken to you.

4 "Abide in Me, and I in you. As the branch cannot bear fruit of itself unless it abides in the vine, so neither can you unless you abide in Me.

• *Mark every reference to **Jesus** with a cross.*

• *Mark every reference to **fruit** with this symbol:* 🍎

• *Put a box around every reference to **abide**. If it says "does not abide," then add a slash through the box.*

DISCUSS

• What does Jesus liken himself to? What does He liken the disciples to?

• What did you learn from marking *abide*? What happens to those who abide in Jesus? Be thorough in your answer.

• What happens to those who do not abide in Jesus?

• What proves that a person is a true disciple of Jesus Christ?

• Now think about what you learned in week three of this study about the two gates, two trees, and two men. Here in John 15 you have those who abide and those who, like Judas, do not abide. Do you see any similarities? Where does the broad gate lead? What happens to the tree that does not bear good fruit? What happens to the foolish man? What happens to the branch (disciple) that does not abide?

• If you are a true disciple of Jesus Christ, will you bear fruit? Where will the fruit come from? How will it come?

5 "I am the vine, you are the branches; he who abides in Me and I in him, he bears much fruit, for apart from Me you can do nothing.

6 "If anyone does not abide in Me, he is thrown away as a branch and dries up; and they gather them, and cast them into the fire and they are burned.

7 "If you abide in Me, and My words abide in you, ask whatever you wish, and it will be done for you.

8 "My Father is glorified by this, that you bear much fruit, and so prove to be My disciples."

JOHN 15:16

"You did not choose Me but I chose you, and appointed you that you would go and bear fruit, and that your fruit would remain, so that whatever you ask of the Father in My name He may give to you."

OBSERVE

Leader: Have the group read aloud John 15:16. Jesus is speaking to eleven of the Twelve.

• *Mark every reference to the **disciples.***

• *Mark every reference to **fruit.***

DISCUSS

• What do you learn from these verses about the true disciples of Jesus?

• What do you learn about their fruit?

• What is promised to them?

WRAP IT UP

Now, how has God spoken to you? What has He shown you in these last forty minutes?

How do you feel? What are your questions?

Does your life bear fruit to one degree or another? What is fruit? It is the product of believing and obeying Jesus.

If you have time, spend a few minutes in short, one-sentence prayers telling God what is on your heart in respect to what you have learned.

(If you would like to study the life of Jesus Christ more thoroughly, you would love the *International Inductive Study Series* book on Luke, titled *The Call to Follow Jesus*. Published by Harvest House Publishers, it is a study designed for small groups, Sunday-school classes, home cell groups, or individual study. It requires about fifteen minutes of homework a day and includes a weekly discussion.)

WEEK FIVE

We have looked at the call of the disciples, the cost of discipleship, and the commitment of being a disciple. Now we want to look at the commissioning of the disciples—and what it means to us today.

Jesus' hour had come. It was about to become the hour of the disciples. Jesus was about to fulfill the work the Father had given Him to do: leave His disciples and go to the Father.

Yet there was a world of men, women, and children who needed to hear the good news of His death and resurrection. Sins could be forgiven; the power of sin could be broken. People could become new creatures in Christ Jesus—children of God, disciples of the Lord Jesus Christ.

However, before Jesus left, there were vital truths the disciples needed to know. A commissioning needed to take place.

OBSERVE

As Jesus moved across the Kidron Valley to His favorite spot in the Garden of Gethsemane, He knew full well what awaited Him and His disciples. Therefore He used those precious moments to prepare them for the tribulation they would face as His followers—for the disciple was to become like His teacher.

Let's pick up where we left off last week in John 15.

JOHN 15:16-20

16 "You did not choose Me but I chose you, and appointed you that you would go and bear fruit, and that your fruit would remain, so that whatever you ask of the Father in My name He may give to you.

17 "This I command you, that you love one another.

18 "If the world hates you, you know that it has hated Me before it hated you.

19 "If you were of the world, the world would love its own; but because you are not of the world, but I chose you out of the world, because of this the world hates you.

Leader: Read aloud John 15:16-20. Jesus is speaking to the eleven disciples.

- *Mark every pronoun referring to the **disciples** as you have done previously.*
- *Mark the word **love** with a heart and **hate** with a heart and a slash through it, like this:*

DISCUSS

- What do you learn from marking references to the disciples? Move through these verses one by one.

- In verse 20, Jesus reminds them that "a slave is not greater than his master." Disciples were not above their teacher. What did people do to Jesus during His three and a half years of public ministry?

- Do you think Christians expect to suffer as a follower of Jesus Christ? What brings the suffering?

• Have you ever seen that the more you become like Christ, the closer you follow Him, the more you might suffer simply because you are less and less in step with the culture of the world? Have you experienced this? How?

20 "Remember the word that I said to you, 'A slave is not greater than his master.' If they persecuted Me, they will also persecute you; if they kept My word, they will keep yours also."

• Do you see people being persecuted today because they are living like Jesus—doing what is right before God, sharing His truths, not compromising, not agreeing when to do so would require going against God's Word?

OBSERVE

After Jesus tells the Eleven that the world hated Him, persecuted Him, and would do the same to them, He reminds them that although He is going away, God is sending them a Helper, just like Him. The Helper is the Holy Spirit who will live within them. This is the promise of the Father.

JOHN 15:26-27

26 "When the Helper comes, whom I will send to you from the Father, that is the Spirit of truth who proceeds from the Father, He will testify about Me,

27 and you will testify also, because you have been with Me from the beginning."

Leader: Read aloud John 15:26-27.

- *Mark every reference to the **Helper** with a big **H,** including all synonyms and pronouns.*
- *Mark the word **testify** by underlining it and adding an arrow pointing up: ↑*

DISCUSS

- What do you learn from marking the references to the Helper?

- Of whom does the Spirit bear witness (testify)?

- What were the disciples to do? Testify of whom?

OBSERVE

Leader: *Read aloud John 16:7-14.*

- *Again mark every reference to the **Helper** and the **Spirit**, including pronouns and synonyms.*
- *Mark any reference to the **world**, including pronouns, with a big circle:* ◯

DISCUSS

- What do you learn from marking the references to the Spirit, the Helper?

- Who sends the Helper?

- What has to happen to Jesus before the Helper can be sent?

- Will the Helper come to the world or to the disciples?

- What will He do through the disciples? In the text, number the three things He will convict the world of through the disciples.

JOHN 16:7-14

7 "But I tell you the truth, it is to your advantage that I go away; for if I do not go away, the Helper will not come to you; but if I go, I will send Him to you.

8 "And He, when He comes, will convict the world concerning sin and righteousness and judgment;

9 concerning sin, because they do not believe in Me;

10 and concerning righteousness, because I go to the Father and you no longer see Me;

11 and concerning judgment, because the ruler of this world has been judged.

12 "I have many more things to say to you, but you cannot bear them now.

13 "But when He, the Spirit of truth, comes, He will guide you into all the truth; for He will not speak on His own initiative, but whatever He hears, He will speak; and He will disclose to you what is to come.

14 "He will glorify Me, for He will take of Mine and will disclose it to you."

• What else will the Helper do?

• According to verse 9, why does the Spirit convict the world of sin?

• What did you learn from verse 10 about the Helper's convicting the world concerning righteousness?

• How can the world be convicted of righteousness if Jesus is gone? Is it not through the world's seeing His righteousness *in us*—that we don't live the same way others live in continuous sin?

• Think about this: The world can't see Jesus because He is not here. But He lives in you, and therefore you don't live as you lived before you became His follower. You don't live the way the rest of the world lives. Now you live righteously—you live according to God's standards. Therefore the world is convicted of righteousness by the Holy Spirit in you because they see that it is possible for a man or woman to live life on a higher plane.

• Is the world in general being convicted of
righteousness by the church in general?
What does this tell you about the state of
those who profess to be Christians?

• What did you learn in verse 11 about the
world's being convicted of judgment
through the Helper in us?

• Think about this: When you became a
child of God, a true believer, you moved
from the kingdom of darkness to the kingdom of light. You are no longer under
the dominion of Satan because God has
become your Father. Therefore Satan
has been judged. The ruler of this world
has been judged and no longer has any
power over you. Your sins have been forgiven; therefore Satan's power is broken. You
are seated at the right hand of God above
all power, authority, dominion, and every
name that is named in heaven and earth.

• How can we as followers of Jesus Christ
live so the world is convicted by the
Spirit within us of sin, righteousness, and
judgment? Give some practical ways.

OBSERVE

After Jesus died for the sins of mankind, was buried, and raised from the dead on the third day, He spent the next forty days with His disciples, instructing them about the kingdom of God (Acts 1:3).

Before He left them to go to the Father, He commissioned them.

MATTHEW 28:16-20

16 But the eleven disciples proceeded to Galilee, to the mountain which Jesus had designated.

17 When they saw Him, they worshiped Him; but some were doubtful.

18 And Jesus came up and spoke to them, saying, "All authority has been given to Me in heaven and on earth.

Leader: Read aloud Matthew 28:16-20.

- *Mark every reference to the **disciples** with an arrow underline, as before:*

  ⟶

- *Mark **therefore** with three dots in the shape of a triangle:* ∴

- *Again ask the group to say aloud the words they will mark.*

When that has been done, have the group read through the passage a second time.

- *Circle every* (**all**) *and the word or phrase it modifies.*

- *Also underline all the **verbs** in verses 19-20 that tell what Jesus wants the disciples to do.*

DISCUSS

• What was Jesus commissioning the disciples to do?

• On what basis?

Leader: *Read aloud the Insight Box.*

INSIGHT

The main verb in Matthew 28:19-20 is translated "make disciples." It is in the imperative mood, making it a command. The other verbs—"go," "baptizing," and "teaching"—are all present participles that support or accompany the making of disciples.

• The primary command in this passage is for the disciples *to make disciples.* What is included in the making of disciples?

• What is to be taught?

• What do you learn from marking *all?* Where is *all* used? What is connected with *all*—all what?

19 "Go therefore and make disciples of all the nations, baptizing them in the name of the Father and the Son and the Holy Spirit,

20 teaching them to observe all that I commanded you; and lo, I am with you always, even to the end of the age."

• What is Jesus' promise to His disciples?

• How do you think this passage relates to believers today?

OBSERVE

We talked at the beginning of this lesson about the cost of being His disciple—the persecution, the suffering that accompanies it. Now let's look at the promise Jesus gave His disciples.

MARK 10:28-30

28 Peter began to say to Him, "Behold, we have left everything and followed You."

29 Jesus said, "Truly I say to you, there is no one who has left house or brothers or sisters or mother or father or children or farms, for My sake and for the gospel's sake,

Leader: Read aloud Jesus' words to Peter in Mark 10:28-30 and have the group say the words they will mark.
 • *Mark **left** with a slash.*
 • *Mark **follow** the same way you marked the word "disciple."*

DISCUSS

• What had the disciples left?

- Was this anything less than what Jesus had explained to them when He called them to be His disciples and spelled out the cost?

- What is Jesus' promise? What can a disciple expect to receive? Be thorough in your answer.

- Practically, it's easy to see how the persecutions come, but how does one receive a hundred times as much in houses, brothers, sisters, mothers, children, and farms?

30 but that he will receive a hundred times as much now in the present age, houses and brothers and sisters and mothers and children and farms, along with persecutions; and in the age to come, eternal life."

WRAP IT UP

The disciples, prototypes for the generations to follow, set the paradigm. They were commanded to reproduce themselves in a sense, to produce others like themselves—those who learn, believe, and obey the teachings of the Lord Jesus Christ, the Son of God, for the rest of their days upon this earth.

The way is narrow, the gate is small, but it leads to eternal life. Jesus set clear parameters. He did not hold back the cost. In this life the cost would be great, but the apostle Paul would later write that the "momentary, light affliction is producing for us an eternal weight of glory far beyond all comparison" (2 Corinthians 4:17).

Although the way of the Cross would bring persecution, they would not walk it alone. Jesus promised to be with His disciples all the way—even to the end of the age.

Now, what has God shown you in these past forty minutes? How has He spoken?

It seems we are truly nearing the "end of the end," and still His faithful disciples unflinchingly follow, many to physical martyrdom. May we, too, be found faithful.

In our final week of study we will see how the disciples carried on the task of making disciples in all nations.

How faithful were the apostles to Jesus' commission to make disciples? Judas, as we've already seen, chose not to continue to abide in Jesus. The others, however, never turned back. Ten of the remaining eleven (all except John, who lived to old age) were put to death for the furtherance of the gospel. Tradition says that John was tortured by being placed in a caldron of hot oil, then he was exiled to the barren Isle of Patmos in the Aegean Sea.

Paul, who was saved after Jesus revealed Himself to him on the road to Damascus, also became an apostle. Personally taught the truth by the resurrected Jesus, Paul, too, was martyred. Beheaded by Rome!

But before these men died, they made disciples so the work of the gospel was carried on—and that work has been carried on from generation to generation, reaching even you.

This week we want to learn some principles of discipleship that can help us in the task God has called us to.

OBSERVE

As we begin, let's go to a passage in Luke and see what Jesus said to those who wanted to follow Him.

Leader: *Read aloud Luke 9:57-62.*
- *Mark the word* ***follow*** *as you marked "disciple."*
- *Circle every reference to the* ***kingdom of God.***

LUKE 9:57-62

57 As they were going along the road, someone said to Him, "I will follow You wherever You go."

58 And Jesus said to him, "The foxes have holes and the birds of the air have nests, but the Son of Man has nowhere to lay His head."

59 And He said to another, "Follow Me." But he said, "Lord, permit me first to go and bury my father."

60 But He said to him, "Allow the dead to bury their own dead; but as for you, go and proclaim everywhere the kingdom of God."

DISCUSS

Obviously the Lord had important principles embodied for us in the telling and preserving of these three occasions. Discuss them incident by incident.

• In verses 57-58, what's the warning, or reality, about following Jesus?

• What happens in the second incident in verses 59-60?

• Is there a sense of timing, of urgency here?

• What was the person to do?

• Do you see any parallels here with what you studied of Jesus' commissioning the Eleven in Matthew 28?

• In the third incident, verses 61-62, what do you learn about looking back instead of moving forward? What do you think it means to look back after putting your hand on the plow?

• Do you see any parallels here with what Jesus said to the multitudes about those who would follow Him as disciples? Any relationship to loving Jesus more than father, mother, brother, sister, children, and your own life?

• Do any of these incidents speak to you in any way? Anything you can learn? Anything that touches a sensitive chord in you?

OBSERVE

Jesus commissioned the disciples to go into all the world and make more disciples, and that is exactly what they did. After Paul had visited and ministered in Thessalonica, he (together with Timothy and Silvanus) wrote a letter to the believers there. In that letter Paul recounted what happened as a result of his visit and the presentation of the gospel. In reading this, we can gain valuable insights into making disciples.

61 Another also said, "I will follow You, Lord; but first permit me to say good-bye to those at home."

62 But Jesus said to him, "No one, after putting his hand to the plow and looking back, is fit for the kingdom of God."

1 Thessalonians 1:5-8

5 For our gospel did not come to you in word only, but also in power and in the Holy Spirit and with full conviction; just as you know what kind of men we proved to be among you for your sake.

6 You also became imitators of us and of the Lord, having received the word in much tribulation with the joy of the Holy Spirit,

7 so that you became an example to all the believers in Macedonia and in Achaia.

Leader: Read aloud 1 Thessalonians 1:5-8.

• *Mark **gospel** and **word** (when it is a synonym for gospel) with a megaphone like this:*

Then have the group read this passage a second time.

• *Circle every pronoun that refers to **Paul, Silvanus,** and **Timothy.***

• *Underline every reference to the **Thessalonians.***

DISCUSS

• According to verse 5, how did the gospel come to the Thessalonians? Number in the text the different ways it came, and discuss them.

• What happened to the Thessalonians as a result of the gospel's coming?

• When the gospel was delivered to the Thessalonians, what accompanied it? Or to put it in other words, how was it received? (*Word* in verse 6 should have been marked with a megaphone.)

• Was this tribulation to be expected?

• What did the Thessalonians become?

• Did they become disciples of Jesus Christ? How do you know, from the verses you just read and marked?

Look at the pattern:

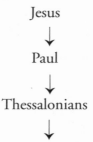

Jesus
↓
Paul
↓
Thessalonians
↓
People in Macedonia and Achaia

8 For the word of the Lord has sounded forth from you, not only in Macedonia and Achaia, but also in every place your faith toward God has gone forth, so that we have no need to say anything.

OBSERVE

In 1 Thessalonians 1:5 you saw that the gospel came by example. The verse says, "You know what kind of men we proved to be among you for your sake."

Let's look at their example. What were they like among them? What can we learn to apply to our own lives?

1 THESSALONIANS 2:1-12

1 For you yourselves know, brethren, that our coming to you was not in vain,

2 but after we had already suffered and been mistreated in Philippi, as you know, we had the boldness in our God to speak to you the gospel of God amid much opposition.

3 For our exhortation does not come from error or impurity or by way of deceit;

4 but just as we have been approved by God to be entrusted with the gospel, so we speak, not as pleasing men, but God who examines our hearts.

5 For we never came with flattering speech,

Leader: Read aloud 1 Thessalonians 2:1-12.
- *Circle every pronoun referring to **Paul, Silvanus,** and **Timothy.***
- *Mark every occurrence of **gospel.***

DISCUSS
- Move verse by verse through the text you just read and discuss what you learn about Paul, Silvanus, and Timothy and how they behaved. What was their example? How did they conduct themselves?

- As you do this, discuss how this could apply to today.

• If you have time, you may want to list your observations under the headings provided.

What They Did

What They Didn't Do

as you know, nor with a pretext for greed—God is witness—

6 nor did we seek glory from men, either from you or from others, even though as apostles of Christ we might have asserted our authority.

7 But we proved to be gentle among you, as a nursing mother tenderly cares for her own children.

8 Having so fond an affection for you, we were well-pleased to impart to you not only the gospel of God but also our own lives, because you had become very dear to us.

9 For you recall, brethren, our labor and hardship, how

working night and day
so as not to be a bur-
den to any of you, we
proclaimed to you the
gospel of God.

10 You are witnesses,
and so is God, how
devoutly and uprightly
and blamelessly we
behaved toward you
believers;

11 just as you know
how we were exhorting
and encouraging and
imploring each one of
you as a father would
his own children,

12 so that you would
walk in a manner wor-
thy of the God who
calls you into His own
kingdom and glory.

OBSERVE

As Paul was facing death for the sake of the gospel, he wrote his last letter to his disciple Timothy, who had become his son in the faith.

Leader: Read aloud 2 Timothy 3:10-14 as Paul reminds his son in the gospel of their relationship.
- *Put a circle around every reference to* **Paul**—*every* **I, me,** *and* **my.**
- *Put a box around every reference to* **Timothy.**
- *Mark* **followed** *with an arrow underline, as you marked "disciple."*

DISCUSS

- What do you see in these verses that parallels what you learned about discipleship—following Jesus Christ? Think about all those things that were to characterize a disciple—and the things a true disciple should expect and should do.

- According to verse 12, what did Paul want Timothy to be sure to understand?

2 TIMOTHY 3:10-14

10 Now you followed my teaching, conduct, purpose, faith, patience, love, perseverance,

11 persecutions, and sufferings, such as happened to me at Antioch, at Iconium and at Lystra; what persecutions I endured, and out of them all the Lord rescued me!

12 Indeed, all who desire to live godly in Christ Jesus will be persecuted.

13 But evil men and impostors will proceed from bad to worse, deceiving and being deceived.

14 You, however, continue in the things you have learned and become convinced of, knowing from whom you have learned them.

2 TIMOTHY 2:1-7

¹ You therefore, my son, be strong in the grace that is in Christ Jesus.

² The things which you have heard from me in the presence of many witnesses, entrust these to faithful men who will be able to teach others also.

³ Suffer hardship with me, as a good soldier of Christ Jesus.

⁴ No soldier in active service entangles himself in the affairs of everyday life, so that he may please the one who enlisted him as a soldier.

• Do you think Christians in general understand this? Why or why not?

OBSERVE

Leader: Read aloud 2 Timothy 2:1-7.
   • *Circle every reference to **Paul.***
   • *Put a box around every reference to **Timothy.***

DISCUSS

Remember that this was Paul's final letter to Timothy, his disciple. Like Jesus, Paul knew he was going to die.

• What do you read that shows how "making disciples" continues from one to another?

• What kind of men was Timothy to choose?

• What are the specific truths Paul wants to drive home in verses 3-6? What is the point he makes by mentioning the soldier, athlete, and farmer?

• Are there any principles in these seven verses that correlate with what you learned about being a disciple these past six weeks? What are they?

OBSERVE

Leader: *Read aloud Acts 11:26.*
  • *Mark the word* **Christians** *with a cross and put a circle around the cross.*
  • *Mark the word* **disciples.**

Leader: *Read aloud the Insight Box.*

INSIGHT

The Greek word for *Christians* is *Christianous*, which simply means "followers of Christ." It is taken from the word *Christos*, which corresponds to the Hebrew word *Messiah*, meaning "the anointed one."

5 Also if anyone competes as an athlete, he does not win the prize unless he competes according to the rules.

6 The hard-working farmer ought to be the first to receive his share of the crops.

7 Consider what I say, for the Lord will give you understanding in everything.

ACTS 11:26

And when he had found him, he brought him to Antioch. And for an entire year they met with the church and taught considerable numbers; and the disciples were first called Christians in Antioch.

DISCUSS

• What do you learn from marking *disciples* and *Christians*?

In our study we saw that people became followers of Jesus Christ but some eventually walked away—ceased to follow Jesus. This is explained in 1 John 2:19: "They went out from us, but they were not really of us; for if they had been of us, they would have remained with us; but they went out, so that it would be shown that they all are not of us." Remember true disciples continue...abide...and bear fruit.

• Do you think a person can be a *true* Christian and not be a *true* disciple of Jesus Christ? Give the reasons for your answer.

• If a person loves Jesus Christ—will he or she obey Him? follow Him?

• And what would He have you to do?

WRAP IT UP

What more can be said, beloved? You have been confronted with truth. You have studied the words of the One who denied Himself and went to the cross—for your redemption. You know what He expects.

Truth always brings us to a crossroad, the crossroad of faith. Will you believe and obey—or walk your own way?

If you choose life, then know, dear one, that you will go through a small narrow gate—but it will lead to eternal life. You will bear good fruit—fruit that will remain. You will have built your house on the Rock—and no storm will move it. It will hold, because you not only hear His words but you do them. Press on, valiant ones.

> *The Lord GOD has given Me the tongue of disciples,*
> *That I may know how to sustain the weary one with a word.*
> *He awakens Me morning by morning,*
> *He awakens My ear to listen as a disciple.*
> ISAIAH 50:4

What a good verse to memorize or to write out and put someplace where you will see it often.

(If you would like to study the book of Acts—which shows the disciples in action, being His witnesses in the power of the Holy Spirit—you would profit like tens of thousands of others from the *International Inductive Study Series* book on Acts titled *The Holy Spirit Unleashed in You.*)

This unique Bible study series from Kay Arthur and the teaching team of Precept Ministries International tackles the issues with which inquiring minds wrestle—in short, easy-to-grasp lessons ideal for small-group settings. These first five study courses in the series can be followed in any order. Here is one possible sequence:

How Do You Know God's Your Father?

by Kay Arthur, David and BJ Lawson

This six-week study looks at the change that takes place when a mortal human encounters a holy God. It focuses on John—who went from being a "son of thunder" to being "the disciple Jesus loved." The student will walk through the book of 1 John, taking note of the characteristics of a child of God versus those of a child of the devil.

Having a Real Relationship with God

by Kay Arthur

For those who yearn to know God and relate to Him in meaningful ways, Kay Arthur opens the Bible to show the way to salvation. With a straightforward examination of vital Bible passages, this enlightening study focuses on where we stand with God, how our sin keeps us from knowing Him, and how Christ bridged the chasm between humans and their Lord.

Being a Disciple: Counting the Real Cost

by Kay Arthur, Tom and Jane Hart

Jesus calls His followers to be disciples. And discipleship comes with a cost, a commitment. This study takes an inductive look at how the

Bible describes a disciple, sets forth the marks of a follower of Christ, and invites students to accept the challenge and then enjoy the blessings of discipleship.

How Do You Walk the Walk You Talk?

by Kay Arthur

This thorough, inductive study of Ephesians 4 and 5 is designed to help students see for themselves what God says about the lifestyle of a true believer in Jesus Christ. The study will equip them to live in a manner worthy of their calling, with the ultimate goal of developing a daily walk with God marked by maturity, Christlikeness, and peace.

Living a Life of True Worship

by Kay Arthur, Bob and Diane Vereen

Worship is one of Christianity's most misunderstood topics. This study explores what the Bible says about worship—what it is, when it happens, where it takes place. Is it based on your emotions? Is it something that only happens on Sunday in church? Does it impact how you serve? This study offers fresh, biblical answers.

ABOUT KAY ARTHUR AND PRECEPT MINISTRIES INTERNATIONAL

Kay Arthur, executive vice president and cofounder of Precept Ministries International, is known around the world as a Bible teacher, author, conference speaker, and host of national radio and television programs.

Kay and her husband, Jack, founded Precept Ministries in 1970 in Chattanooga, Tennessee. Started as a fledgling ministry for teens, Precept today is a worldwide outreach that establishes children, teens, and adults in God's Word, so that they can discover the Bible's truths for themselves. Precept inductive Bible studies are taught in all 50 states. The studies have been translated into 65 languages, reaching 118 countries.

Kay is the author of more than 120 books and inductive Bible study courses, with a total of over 5 million books in print. She is sought after by groups throughout the world as an inspiring Bible teacher and conference speaker. Kay is also well known globally through her daily and weekly television and radio programs.

Contact Precept Ministries International for more information about inductive Bible studies in your area.

Precept Ministries International
P.O. Box 182218
Chattanooga, TN 37422-7218
800-763-8280
www.precept.org

ABOUT TOM AND JANE HART

Tom and Jane Hart direct the Canadian ministry of Precept Ministries International. In addition to being authors, they often speak at churches, Bible colleges, conferences, and retreats across Canada and overseas. Tom, a lawyer, is completing a doctoral degree in ministry. Jane, a nurse, has been a Bible teacher for more than twenty years. Married for thirty-one years, Tom and Jane have three children and two grandchildren. They reside in Brantford, Ontario.